PAUL COOKSON'S
JOKE SHOP

Paul Cookson has been writing poems since he was at school, publishing books since he was eighteen and has worked as a poet for a further twenty-five years.

He has written thousands of poems (not all of them good, but a lot of them funny), visited around 4,000 schools, libraries and festivals, and performed to over a million people.

Poet in Residence at The National Football Museum and Poet Laureate for Slade, Paul was a National Reading Hero in 2009.

Paul is married and lives in Nottinghamshire with two children, a dog and too many ukuleles. His favourite joke-shop item is obviously a whoopee cushion.

You can keep up with latest news about Paul on his website: www.paulcooksonpoet.co.uk

Si Smith used to be a teacher, but he escaped (shh, don't tell anyone) and now he gets paid to draw pictures.

Like Gary Lineker, King Richard III and Engelbert Humperdinck, he is from Leicester.

Si is not as famous as they are but, like them, he is quite old.

Si knows two good jokes. One is very long and about Quasimodo, the Hunchback of Notre-Dame. The other is a 'knock, knock' joke about an interrupting cow. He also knows a rubbish joke about a lobster.

Si likes cake, curry, football and drawing aliens. He dislikes celery, cranberries and drawing cats or violins.

Follow Si on: www.simonsmithillustrator.co.uk

PAUL COOKSON'S JOKE SHOP

ILLUSTRATED BY SI SMITH

MACMILLAN CHILDREN'S BOOKS

First published 2014 by Macmillan Children's Books
a division of Macmillan Publishers Limited
20 New Wharf Road, London N1 9RR
Basingstoke and Oxford
Associated companies throughout the world
www.panmacmillan.com

ISBN 978-1-4472-5465-2

1 3 5 7 9 8 6 4 2

A CIP catalogue record for this book is available from
the British Library.

Printed and bound by CPI Group (UK) Ltd, Croydon CR0 4YY

For Mum, Sally, Sam and Daisy

As a man of several double acts,
these poems are also for David Harmer,
Stewart Henderson and Stan Cullimore

'Wordsmithery of the highest order and wittiest bent' – Mark Radcliffe

'Simple, direct and poetic. Caring, compassionate and funny' – Ian McMillan

'As funny as ever – always a festival highlight' – Northern Children's Book Festival

'An abundance of jests, jokes and japes – like the *Beano* in poetry form' – *Junior Education*

'They tell me he's a Reading Hero – after reading his (football) poems, he's my hero too' – Bill Kenwright

'Read on and I guarantee that you won't be disappointed' – Noddy Holder

'Every day should have a Paul Cookson moment in it. Keep him by your bedside for emergencies' – Simon Mayo

'Funny, witty, clever, wise – just four of many words I could use to describe the poems of Paul Cookson. (I do know a lot more words but some of them are heavy and might slide off the page.) More important than anything I might say is the fact that children love them – and children can't be fooled. They smell a 'wrong-un' at a hundred miles (because their noses are really that long). So enjoy this book, from the wonderful daftness of 'Superman's Dog' to the sad truth of 'It's Not the Same Any More'; and enjoy all the poems in between and beyond whether you are a grown-up of eight or a child of eighty – cos it's all GOOD STUFF!' – Mike Harding

CONTENTS

INTRODUCTION

Hello and welcome to my Joke Shop.

If someone had told me twenty-five years ago that I'd make a living as a poet, visit around four thousand schools, travel the world, sell over a million books and that I'd have met some of my heroes, I'm not sure I'd have believed them. But here we are. And all because of poetry.

If I was a rock star (and part of me once wanted to be) this would be my 'greatest hits' album. Some of these poems have been with me for all those twenty-five years, while others are newer favourites.

They are all collected together for the first time and brilliantly illustrated and brought to life by Simon Smith.

Thanks to John, Mike, Simon and Noddy for the fantastic quotes on the back. Special thanks also to my wife and family for putting up with my constant travels and for letting me out to play. Respect to all the poets who I've worked alongside and been inspired by over the years, and to Gaby Morgan – long-standing editor and friend. And of course to the schools, librarians, festivals and constant book-buyers. You are all stars.

A long time ago, when I was still at school, I sang along with a famous song, and still those words ring true: 'Look to the future now, it's only just begun . . .'

Let's hope that the Joke Shop stays open for another twenty-five years.

Paul Cookson

LET NO ONE STEAL YOUR DREAMS

Let no one steal your dreams
Let no one tear apart
The burning of ambition
That fires the drive inside your heart

Let no one steal your dreams
Let no one tell you that you can't
Let no one hold you back
Let no one tell you that you won't

Set your sights and keep them fixed
Set your sights on high
Let no one steal your dreams
Your only limit is the sky

Let no one steal your dreams
Follow your heart
Follow your soul
For only when you follow them
Will you feel truly whole

Set your sights and keep them fixed
Set your sights on high
Let no one steal your dreams
Your only limit is the sky

MUM USED PRITT STICK

Mum used Pritt Stick
Instead of lipstick
Then went and kissed my dad

Two days passed
Both stuck fast
The longest snog they ever had

BOUNCY MR SPRINGER

BOING! BOING!
            BA-DOING BOING BOING!

He bounces when he walks
And he bounces when he talks
He bounces down the corridor
Up and down on the school hall floor
Up and down on the school hall floor

BOING! BOING!
            BA-DOING BOING BOING!

Up and down he bounces round
And points his bouncy finger
Best watch out when he's about
It's bouncy Mister Springer

BOING! BOING!
    BA-DOING BOING BOING!

He bounces in assembly
His rubber knees are trembly
You can tell where he has been
He's a human trampoline
A jumping bean on a trampoline

BOING! BOING!
    BA-DOING BOING BOING!

He bounces here, bounces there
And he bounces . . . everywhere
Bounces on the tables, bounces on the chairs
Bounces in his clothes and in his . . . underwear (not
  really!)

He bounces round the classroom
He bounces to the staffroom
He's a human kangaroo
He even bounces on the loo
Up and down on the staffroom loo!

BOING! BOING!
    BA-DOING BOING BOING!

A SIGHT FOR PAW EYES

Our pets like to plan a joke surprise
The cat has spectacles with googly eyes
The dogs have both got glasses
With false noses and moustaches
And the parrot and the budgie wear bow ties

THE KING OF ALL THE DINOSAURS

With taloned feet and razor claws,
Leathery scales, monstrous jaws
The king of all the dinosaurs
Tyrannosaurus ... Rex!

With sabre teeth no one ignores,
It rants and raves and royally roars
The king of all the dinosaurs
Tyrannosaurus ... Rex!

The largest of the carnivores,
It stomps and chomps on forest floors
The king of all the dinosaurs
Tyrannosaurus ... Rex!

Charges forwards, waging wars,
Gouges, gorges, gashes, gores
The king of all the dinosaurs
Tyrannosaurus ... Rex!

With taloned feet and razor claws,
Leathery scales, monstrous jaws
The king of all the dinosaurs
Tyrannosaurus ... Rex!

PANTS ON FIRE

I can change a tractor tyre
Visit hobbits in the shire
Balance high upon a wire
Liar liar – Pants on fire!
Liar liar – Pants on fire!

I can't stand this heating
Driving me insane
Wherever I am seating
My bottom is in pain
Feel the flames reaching higher
Ooh! Aah! Pants on fire!
Ooh! Aah! Pants on fire!

Pants on fire! Pants on fire!
Liar liar – Pants on fire!

I can climb the highest spire
Sing in tune in the choir
Bite the neck of a big vampire
Liar liar – Pants on fire!
Liar liar – Pants on fire!

I am always fuming
Butt it is no joke
Big black clouds ballooning

Swirling plumes of smoke
Glowing in this strange attire
Ooh! Aah! Pants on fire!
Ooh! Aah! Pants on fire!

Pants on fire! Pants on fire!
Liar liar – Pants on fire!

Always in the hot seat
Wherever I am going
The scorching and the torching
My rear is always glowing
Hotter than a deep-fat-fryer
Glowing in this strange attire
Feel the flames reaching higher
Ooh! Aah! Pants on fire!
Ooh! Aah! Pants on fire!

INVISIBLE MAGICIANS

Thanks be to all magicians
The ones we never see
Who toil away both night and day
Weaving spells for you and me

The ones who paint the rainbows
The ones who salt the seas
The ones who purify the dew
And freshen up the breeze

The who brighten lightning
The ones who whiten snow
The ones who shine the sunshine
And give the moon its glow

The ones who buff the fluffy clouds
And powder blue the skies
The ones who splash the colours on
The sunset and sunrise

The ones who light volcanoes
The ones who soak the showers
The ones who wave the waves
And open up the flowers

The ones who spring the Spring
And warm the Summer air
The ones who carpet Autumn
And frost the Winter earth

The ones who polish icicles
The ones who scatter stars
The ones who cast their magic spells
Upon this world of ours

Thanks to one and thanks to all
Invisible and true
Nature's magic – heaven sent
To earth for me and you.

MORE ELECTRICITY VICAR?

Everything went just as I had planned
Thanks to the buzzer in my hand
I shook hands with the vicar
His eyes began to flicker
And he jumped around like a rubber band

BARRY AND BERYL THE BUBBLEGUM BLOWERS

Barry and Beryl the bubblegum blowers
Blew bubblegum bubbles as big as balloons
All shapes and sizes, zebras and Zeppelins
Swordfish and sea lions, sharks and baboons
Babies and buckets, bottles and biplanes
Buffaloes, bees, trombones and bassoons
Barry and Beryl the bubblegum blowers
Blew bubblegum bubbles as big as balloons

Barry and Beryl the bubblegum blowers
Blew bubblegum bubbles all over the place
Big ones in bed, on back seats of buses
Blowing their bubbles in baths with bad taste
They blew and they bubbled from breakfast till bedtime
The biggest gum bubble that history traced
One last big breath . . . and the bubble exploded
Bursting and blasting their heads into space
Yes, Barry and Beryl the bubblegum blowers
Blew bubbles that blasted their heads into space

SUPERMAN'S DOG

Superman's dog – he's the best
Helping pets in distress
Red and gold pants and vest
'SD' on his chest

Superman's dog – X-ray sight
Green bones filled with kryptonite
Bright blue Lycra tights in flight
Faster than a meteorite

Better than Batman's robin
Rougher than Robin's bat
Faster than Spider-Man's spider
Cooler than Catwoman's cat

Superman's dog – bionic scent
Crime prevention – his intent
Woof and tough – cement he'll dent
What's his name – Bark Kent!

SHORT VISIT, LONG STAY

Our school trip was a special occasion
But we never reached our destination
Instead of the zoo
I was locked in the loo
On an M62 service station

BOTTOMS!

Bottoms! Bottoms!
Children – on your bottoms!
Bottoms! Bottoms!
Children – on your bottoms!

Lots of bottoms through the door
Lots of bottoms on the floor
Lots of bottoms wall to wall
Lots of bottoms fill the hall
Bottoms that are wriggling
Bottoms that are wiggling
Bottoms that are slithering
Fidgeting and jiggling

Bottoms that are twitching
Bottoms that are itching
Bottoms that are slipping
Bottoms that are tipping
Wobblebottoms, jelly bottoms
Wrigglebottoms, smelly bottoms

Bottoms that are jumping
Bottoms that are pumping
Bottoms that are loud bottoms
Stand-out-in-the-crowd bottoms
Cheeky bottoms, sneaky bottoms
Squeaky bottoms, leaky bottoms

Bouncy bottoms left and right
Bouncy bottoms side to side
Bouncy bottoms up and down
Bouncy bottoms round and round

There's no chance of stopping
This bottom body-popping
Their memories are rotten
So they have all forgotten

ON YOUR BOTTOMS!

Don't wriggle
Don't wiggle
Don't twitch
Don't itch
Don't jump
Don't pump
Don't slip
Don't tip
Don't squeak
Don't sneak
Don't parp
Don't start

Boys! Boys! No bottom noise!
Don't be rude! Do not move!
Don't move a muscle till – teachers say you will
Don't move until – Please just sit still!

Bottoms! Bottoms!
Children – on your bottoms
Bottoms! Bottoms!
Children – ON – YOUR – BOTTOMS!!!

WHOA! NO! BOA!

Cousin Jim took the top right off the tin
That he thought had nuts and raisins in
You should have heard him shout
When the snake flew out
Smacking cousin Jim upon his chin

THE TOILET SEAT HAS TEETH

The bathroom has gone crazy
Far beyond belief
The sink is full of spiders
And the toilet seat has teeth!

The plughole in the bath
Has a whirlpool underneath
That pulls you down feet first
And the toilet seat has teeth!

The toothpaste tube is purple
And makes your teeth fall out.
The toilet roll is nettles
And makes you scream and shout!

The towels have got bristles
The bubble bath is glue
The soap has turned to jelly
And it makes your skin bright blue.

The mirror's pulling faces
At everyone it can
The shower's dripping marmalade
And blackcurrant jam.

The rubber ducks are breeding
And building their own nest
With shaving foam and tissues
In Grandad's stringy vest.

Shampoo is liquid dynamite
There's petrol in the hairspray
Both will cure dandruff
When they blow your head away!

The bathroom has gone crazy
Far beyond belief
The sink is full of spiders
And the toilet seat has teeth!

The toilet seat has teeth! Ow!
The toilet seat has teeth! Ow!
The toilet seat has teeth! Ow!
The toilet seat has teeth! Ow!

Crunch! Slurp! Munch! Burp!
The toilet seat has teeth! Ow!
Don't – sit – on – it!
The toilet seat has . . . !
   Owwwww!

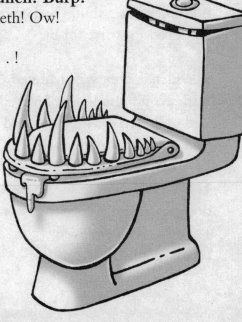

PARENTS' EVENING

Better get away and get away quick
Mum and Dad are soppy and I feel sick
But I can't get away, I feel so harassed
Mum and Dad are snogging and I'm so embarrassed

It started with Dad tickling Mum
And then she couldn't stop wriggling
Then he whispered something rude
And soon they both were giggling

Before too long she held his hand
And then he stroked her knee
A moment later things had gone
From bad to worse for me ...

The silence then was shattered
With a loud resounding SMACK!
Dad puckered – Mum suckered
And began the snog attack

They didn't seem to breathe at all
But gasped and gulped mid kiss
Their lips forever sealed
Like two glued jellyfish

All that squashing, all the squelching
All that slurpy sloshing
All the dripping, all the drooling,
Everyone was watching

It wouldn't have been so bad
If the room was dark and dull
But it was my Parents' Evening
The hall was lit . . . and jam-packed full

If no one knew my mum and dad
Then I wouldn't have to worry
But Dad is the headmaster
And Mum's the secretary!

MISS KING'S KONG

It was our 'Bring your pet to school' day . . .

Warren's wolfhound was chasing Paula's poodle
Paula's poodle was chasing Colin's cat
Colin's cat was chasing Harriet's hamster
And Harriet's hamster was chasing Benny's beetle.

Suzie's snake was trying to swallow
Freddie's frog, Percy's parrot, Rebecca's rabbit,
Belinda's bat, Gordon's goat, Peter's pig
And part of Patricia's pony

When all of a sudden everything stopped.

Miss King had brought her pet to school as well.
Miss King's Kong stood there, roared and beat his
    chest.

Miss King smiled.
Miss King's Kong smiled too
As he swung from the light, eating bananas.

Everything was quiet
Until the headmaster came in with his pet . . .
Mr Lock's Ness was a real monster.

OUR TEACHER'S MOST UNFAVOURITE CREATURES

Mrs Richards wasn't that impressed
With the rubber snake upon her desk
The bat we hung down from the door
Made her leap up even more
Then she saw the spider on her dress!

WHERE TEACHERS KEEP THEIR PETS

Mrs Cox has a fox
Nesting in her curly locks.

Mr Spratt's tabby cat
Sleeps beneath his bobble hat.

Mrs Cahoots has various newts
Swimming in her zip-up boots.

Mr Spry has Fred his fly
Eating food stains from his tie.

Mrs Groat shows off her stoat
Round the collar of her coat.

Mr Spare's got grizzly bears
Hiding in his big wide flares.

And . . .

Mrs Vickers has a stick insect called 'Stickers'
And she keeps it in her . . .

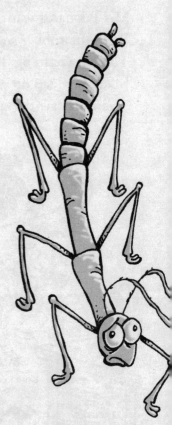

IT'S NOT THE SAME ANY MORE

It's not the same since Patch died.
Sticks are just sticks.
Never thrown, never fetched.

It's not the same any more.
Tennis-balls lie still and lifeless.
The urge to bounce them has gone.

It's not the same now.
I can't bring myself to whistle.
There's no reason to do so.

His collar hangs on the hook
And his name tag and lead are dusty.

His basket and bowl are in a plastic bag
Lying at an angle on a garage shelf.

My new slippers will never be chewed
And I've no excuse for my lack of homework any more.

I can now watch the football in peace, uninterrupted.
No frantic barking and leaping just when it gets to the
    goal.

I don't have to share my sweets and biscuits
And then wipe the dribbling drool off my trouser legs.

It's just not the same any more.
When Patch died a small part of me died too.

All that's left is a mound of earth
And my hand-made cross beneath the apple tree.

All that's left are memories.
Thousands of them.

It's just not the same any more.

SEA SHOALS SEE SHOWS ON THE SEABED

The salmon with a hat on was conducting with a baton
It tried to tune a tuna fish by playing on its scales
The scales had all been flattened when the tuna fish
    was sat on
On purpose by a porpoise and a school of killer whales
So the salmon with a hat on fiddled with his baton
The angelfish got ready to play the tambourine
Things began to happen when the salmon with a baton
Was tapping out a pattern for the band of the marines

There was a minnow on piano, a prawn with a horn
An otter on guitar looking all forlorn
A whale-voice choir and a carp with a harp
A belly-dancing jellyfish jiving with a shark

The octaves on the octopus played the middle eight
But they couldn't keep in time with the skiffle-playing
    skate
The plaice on the bass began to rock and roll
With the bloater in a boater and a Dover sole

A clam on castanets, an eel on glockenspiel
An oyster in a cloister singing with a seal
The haddock had a headache from the deafening din
And the sword-dancing swordfish sliced off a fin

A limpet on a trumpet, flatfish on a flute
The kipper fell asleep with King Canute
Barracuda on a tuba sat upon a rock
The electric eel gave everyone a shock

The shrimp and the sturgeon, the stingray and the squid
Sang a four-part harmony on the seabed
The crab and the lobster gave their claws a flick
Kept everyone in time with a click click click . . .
Kept everyone in time with a click click click . . .
Kept everyone in time with a click click click . . .

Yes, the salmon with a hat on was tapping out a pattern
And things began to happen for the band of the marines
It was an ocean of commotion of Atlantic proportion
The greatest show by schools of shoals that ever had
    been seen

TARANTULATOR

Half alien creature, half machine
Eyes that glow both red and green
Robot spider terminator
Look out – Tarantulator!

Eight long legs – multi-jointed
Spikes and spots – poisoned, pointed
Predatory aggravator
Look out – Tarantulator!

Venom in those vampire fangs
Do not feel those hunger pangs
Threads and webs of steel creator
Look out – Tarantulator!

Radioactive hairs that quiver
Saliva like an acid river
Interspecies space mutator
Look out – Tarantulator!

It'll be back – to see you later
Look out ! Tarantulator!

THE MONSTER SPIDER ON THE CEILING

Watching, waiting, way up high
Loitering with evil eye
For that moment of revealing
The monster spider on the ceiling

Pupils sitting in the hall
Assemble while it starts to crawl
Step by step, most unappealing
The monster spider on the ceiling

Like a dark cloud in the blue
Eventually comes into view
There's no hiding or concealing
The monster spider on the ceiling

One by one, all realize
With open mouths and widened eyes
Pointing, panicking and squealing
The monster spider on the ceiling

Shrieking, shouting as it's crawling
Frightened that it may start falling
The assembled trembled, senses reeling
The monster spider on the ceiling

To the rescue, one brave teacher
On a chair reached to the creature
One swift move and she was peeling
The monster spider from the ceiling

With a pint glass from the staffroom
And some cardboard from the classroom
Very soon she was dealing
With that monster on the ceiling

Safely, soundly, slowly, surely
The creepy caught by Mrs Crawley
She relieved all anxious feeling
Caught the monster on the ceiling

Took it out across the yard
To the fence and chucked it hard
Somersaulting and cartwheeling
Bye bye spider from the ceiling!

FOUR CRAZY PETS

I've four crazy pets, all rather jolly —
Rover, Tiddles, Flopsy and Polly
A dog, a rabbit, a parrot and a cat
Which one's which? Can you guess that?

Rover's a dog? No!
Tiddles is a cat? No!
Flopsy's a rabbit? No!
Polly's a parrot? No!

My dog has the appetite of a small gorilla
We call her *Polly* cos we can never *filla*

The rabbit has a habit of wetting where we're standing
We call him *Tiddles* cos the puddles keep expanding

Our cat purrs like an engine turning over
Vroom vroom vroom — so we call her *Rover*

The fact that our parrot cannot fly is such a shame
Flopsy by nature and *Flopsy* by name

Four crazy names! Wouldn't you agree?
I think my pets fit their names *purr*fectly

EYE SAY EYE SAY EYE SAY

The trick upon our Head – it proved most popular
I was only trying to be jocular
Ink on a telescope
Is a very ancient joke
So instead I went and used binoculars!

HE JUST CAN'T KICK IT WITH HIS FOOT

John from our team
Is a goalscoring machine
Phenomenally mesmerizing but . . .
The sport is called football
Yet his boots don't play at all
Cos he just can't kick it with his foot

He can skim it from his shin
He can spin it on his chin
He can nod it in the net with his nut
He can blow it with his lips
Or skip it off his hips
But he just can't kick it with his foot

With simplicity and ease
He can use his knobbly knees
To blast it past the keeper, both eyes shut
He can whip it up and flick it
With his tongue and lick it
But he just can't kick it with his foot

Overshadowing the best
With the power from his chest
Like a rocket from a socket he can put
The ball into the sack
With a scorcher from his back
But he just can't kick it with his foot

Baffling belief
With the ball between his teeth
He can dribble his way out of any rut
Hypnotize it with his eyes
Keep it up on both his thighs
But he just can't kick it with his foot

From his shoulder to his nose
He can juggle it and pose
With precision and incision he can cut
Defences straight in half
With a volley from his calf
But he just can't kick it with his foot

He can keep it off the deck
Bounce the ball upon his neck
With his ball control you should see him strut
He can flap it with both ears
To loud applause and cheers
But he just can't kick it with his foot

He can trap it with his tum
Direct it with his bum
Deflect it just by wobbling his gut
When he's feeling silly
He can even use his . . . ankle!
But he just can't kick it with his foot

THE GOALIE WITH EXPANDING HANDS

Any crosses, any shots
I will simply stop the lot
I am always in demand
The goalie with expanding hands

Volleys, blasters, scissor kicks
I am safe between the sticks
All attacks I will withstand
The goalie with expanding hands

Free kicks or a penalty
No one ever scores past me
Strong and bold and safe I'll stand
The goalie with expanding hands

Let their strikers be immense
I'm the last line of defence
Alert, on duty, all posts manned
The goalie with expanding hands

Palms as long as arms expand
Thumbs and fingers ready fanned
You may as well shoot in the stand
Not a chance! Understand?

Number one in all the land
Superhuman, super-spanned
In control and in command
I'm the man, I'm the man
The one and only goalie . . . with my expanding hands

DAD'S HAT-TRICK CELEBRATIONS

When Dad scored a goal in the garden
He celebrated with glee
He put his T-shirt over his head
And ran into the tree!

When he scored his second
He should have had more sense
He tried to slide but couldn't stop
And smashed the garden fence!

His hat-trick handstand antics tried
To claim the ball and grab it
He slipped and tripped, his trousers ripped
And he flattened next door's rabbit!

When Mum came out and shouted
It was me he blamed
But luckily I'd filmed it
Now it's been on *You've Been Framed!*

FOOTY LOOKALIKES

Grandad thinks he's Bobby Charlton –
   Just because he's bald
Uncle thinks he's Peter Crouch –
   Because he's really tall
Just because he wears a cap –
   Dad think he's Petr Čech
Brother thinks he's Rooney –
   Because he looks like Shrek

THE FOOTBALLER'S PRAYER

Our team
Which art eleven
Hallowed be thy game
Our match be won
Their score be none
On turf as we score . . . at least seven
Give us today – no daily red . . . card
And forgive us our lost passes
As we forgive those
Who lose passes against us
Lead us not into retaliation
And deliver us from penalties
For three is the kick off
The power and scorer
For ever and ever
Full time

DO AS YOU ARE TOLD! (PARENTS)

44

45

46

MUM FOR A DAY

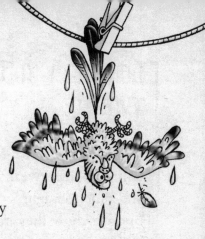

Mum's ill in bed today
So I said I'd do the housework
And look after things
She told me it was really hard
But I said it would be dead easy
So . . .

I hoovered the sink
Dusted the cat
Cooked Dad's shoes and socks in a pie
Washed up the carpet in the dishwasher
Fed the ornaments
Polished the fish, chips and mushy peas
Ironed the letters and parcels
Posted the shirts and knickers
And . . . last of all . . .
Hung the budgie out to dry.

It took me all day but I got everything finished
And I was really tired
And I'm really glad Mum isn't ill every day.
So is the budgie.

DON'T GET YOUR KNICKERS IN A TWIST!

We never knew that Mum could be a great contortionist
Until the underwear she wore decided to resist
She aimed straight for the leg holes
But somehow they missed . . .
In a spot, the day she got her knickers in a twist.

They restricted and constricted her like an iron fist
Held hostage by the tightening elastic terrorist
With one leg round her head
And the other near her wrist
A human knot, the day she got her knickers in a twist.

She struggled, strained and wrestled
But they would not desist
The wrangling and the strangling continued to persist
Walking like an alien
Exhibitionist
A hop, a squat, a trot, she's got her kickers in a twist.

Trussed up like a chicken
Peering through her legs she hissed
'Help me, quick! What I need's a physiotherapist!'
Dad's reply was casual and utterly dismissed
When he said 'Do not fret
There's no need to panic . . . yet
Play it cool, just don't get . . . your knickers in a twist.'

TEENAGE BROTHER'S BEDROOM FLOOR

Spot the carpets, find the smell
Which is which? Who can tell?
It's all camouflaged so well
Things are left just where they fell
Notes are written in the dust
A mountain range of pizza crusts
What's behind the dreaded door?
Teenage brother's bedroom floor

Yogurt pots and spoons that stick
Congealing like an oil slick
Piles of clothes, metres thick
Like the wardrobe has been sick
The aftermath of a tsunami
Dirty washing for an army
A battlefield, a lazy war
Teenage brother's bedroom floor

Magazines he hasn't read
Dirty quilt and unmade bed
Bits of toast and mouldy bread

One bike wheel from the shed
A thousand scrunched up biscuit packets
Pocket contents from his jackets
Like a shipwreck washed ashore
Teenage brother's bedroom floor

Trainers from another time
T-shirts stained with grease and grime
Socks with slugs and snails that climb
Up walls while leaving trails of slime
The underpants that time forgot
Left to fester, left to rot
What is worse – a cesspit or
Teenage brother's bedroom floor

Homework that he's never done
Blobs of dried up chewing gum
School letters not seen by Mum
Curtains closing out the sun
Permanently lost in gloom
Darkened shadows shroud the room
A million secrets, maybe more
Teenage brother's bedroom floor

A football sock with last year's mud
A football shirt with last year's blood
A football boot without a stud
A punctured football that's no good
Trainer laces, one shin pad
Swimming towel, mouldy bag
Banana skins and apple core
Teenage brother's bedroom floor

Videos and cheap CDs
Cases lacking DVDs
Controllers for PS3s
Games consoles and things like these
Leads for charging mobile phones
Knotted wires, traffic cones
Like a burgled junk-shop store
Teenage brother's bedroom floor

Setting gel no longer sealed
Dripped and dribbled and congealed
Furry orange – nearly peeled
Every surface is concealed

Crumbs from crisps and crinkled chips
Topless pens and dry felt-tips
Smells and sights you can't ignore
Teenage brother's bedroom floor

For years and years and years it's been a
No-go crime scene misdemeanour
Splattered Coke and spilt Ribena
Never seen a vacuum cleaner
It's a zone that's adult free
Guaranteed for privacy
Surely it's against the law
Teenage brother's bedroom floor

It's a toxic situation
Needing total fumigation
Quarantine and isolation
From osmosis and mutation
Evolution carries on
It's all linked and joined as one
Can't tell what it was before
Teenage brother's bedroom floor

JUST MUM AND ME

We didn't do anything special today,
Just Mum and me.
Raining outside, nowhere to go,
Just Mum and me.

So we baked and talked and talked and baked
And baked and talked,
Just Mum and me.

She told me about when she was young
And how her gran baked exactly the same cakes
On rainy days and baked and talked to her.

She remembered her friends
And the games they used to play,
The trees they used to climb,
The fields they used to run around in
And how summers always seemed to be sunny.

And Mum smiled a smile I don't often see,
The years falling away from her face,
And just for a moment
I caught a glimpse of the girl she used to be.

We didn't do anything special today,
Raining outside, nowhere to go,
So we baked and talked and talked and baked,
Just Mum and me.

I ate and listened and listened and ate,
The hours racing by so quickly.

We didn't do anything special . . .
But it was special, really special.

Just Mum and me.

FATHER'S HANDS

Father's hands
Large like frying pans
Broad as shovel blades
Strong as weathered spades.

Father's hands
Finger ends ingrained with dirt
Permanently stained from work
Ignoring pain and scorning hurt.

I once saw him walk boldly up to a swan
That had landed in next door's drive
And wouldn't move.
The police were there
Because swans are a protected species,
But didn't do anything, yet my dad walked up to it,
Picked it up and carried it away. No problem.
Those massive wings that can break a man's bones
Were held tight, tight by my father's hands
And I was proud of him that day, really proud.

Father's hands
Tough as leather on old boots
Firmly grasping nettle shoots
Pulling thistles by their roots.

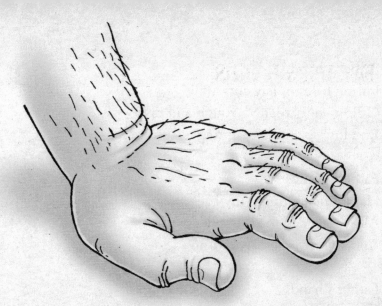

Father's hands
Gripping like an iron vice
Never numb in snow and ice
Nails and screws are pulled and prised.

He once found a kestrel with a broken wing
And kept it in our garage until it was better.
He'd feed it by hand with scraps of meat or dead mice
And you could see where its beak and talons
Had taken bits of skin from his finger ends.
It never seemed to hurt him at all, he just smiled
As he let it claw and peck.

Father's hands
Lifting bales of hay and straw
Calloused, hardened, rough and raw
Building, planting, painting . . . more.

Father's hands
Hard when tanning my backside
All we needed they supplied
And still my hands will fit inside

Father's hands
Large like frying pans
Broad as shovel blades
Strong as weathered spades.

And still my hands could fit inside
My father's hands.

SQUEAK! EEK! LEAP!

The clockwork mouse moves my gran to tears
You should see her face when it appears
We thought she was unable
But she leaped on to the table
It's the fastest that she's moved in fifteen years

CHOP!CHOP!

Grandad keeps his teeth beside the bed
I swapped them for the clockwork ones instead
It was a disaster
As they clattered faster
Flying out past my grandma's head

REVENGE OF THE HAMSTER

No one realized, nobody knew
The hamster was sleeping inside my dad's shoe

He put in his foot and squashed flat its nose
So it opened its jaws and chomped on his toes

While howling and yowling and hopping like mad
The hamster wreaked further revenge on my dad

It scampered and scurried up his trouser leg . . .
And this time bit something much softer instead

His eyes bulged and popped like marbles on stalks
And watered while walking the strangest of walks

His ears wiggled wildly while shooting out steam
All the dogs in the town heard his falsetto scream

His face went deep purple, his hair stood on end
His mouth like a letter box caught in the wind

The hamster's revenge was almost complete . . .
Dad couldn't sit down for several weeks

Now Dad doesn't give our hamster a chance . . .
He wears stainless-steel socks and hamster-proof pants

FULL OF SURPRISES

This poem is full of surprises
Each line holds something new
This poem is full of surprises
Especially for you . . .

It's full of tigers roaring
It's full of loud guitars
It's full of comets soaring
It's full of shooting stars

It's full of pirates fighting
It's full of winning goals
It's full of alien sightings
It's full of rock and roll

It's full of rainbows beaming
It's full of eagles flying
It's full of dreamers dreaming
It's full of teardrops drying

It's full of magic spells
It's full of wizards' pointy hats
It's full of fairy elves
It's full of witches and black cats

It's full of dragons breathing fire
It's full of dinosaurs
It's full of mountains reaching higher
It's full of warm applause

It's full of everything you need
It's full of more besides
It's full of food, the world to feed
It's full of fairground rides

It's full of love and happiness
It's full of dreams come true
It's full of things that are the best
Especially for you

It's jammed and crammed and packed and stacked
With things both old and new
This poem is full of surprises
Especially for you.

LOVE POEM FOR . . .

I just can't wait to be with you
Time flies by when you are there
You take me to another place
Just me and you and a comfy chair

You fill my head with images
And feelings I can't wait to share
You touch all my emotions
Just me and you and a comfy chair

Where you go I follow
You can take me anywhere
Horizons disappear with you . . .
A favourite book and a comfy chair.

MAY YOU ALWAYS

May your smile be ever present
May your skies always be blue
May your path be ever onward
May your heart be ever true

May your dreams be full to bursting
May your steps always be sure
May the fire within your soul
Blaze on for evermore

May you live to meet ambition
May you strive to pass each test
May you find the love your life deserves
May you always have the best

May your happiness be plentiful
May your regrets be few
May you always be my best friend
May you always be . . . just you

HOME ... WORK

Next time your teacher asks you
The dreaded question
Where is your homework?

You can safely say – It's at – home

When they say
So why is your homework at home and not at school?

You can safely say that
The clue is in the title, dear teacher,
Listen to the words you called it ...

Home

Work

Work to be done – at home
Work to leave – at home
Work to stay – at home
That's why it's called – Home-Work

If it was meant for school
It would be called – School-Work
But it's not
It's called – Home-Work

Work to be done – at home
Work you can leave – at home
Work to stay – at home
That's why it's called – Home-Work

If it should be done at home
And brought to school the next day
It would be called
Do-it-at-home-and-bring-it-to-school-the-next-
    day-Work
But it's not
It's called – Home-Work

Work to be done – at home
Work you can leave – at home
Work that can stay – at home
That's why it's called – Home-Work

You've done it – at home
You've left it – at home
That's where it should be – at home
Because it's called . . .
HOME-WORK!!!!!

MRS EAGLE'S EYES

Eyes, eyes – Mrs Eagle's eyes
Eyes, eyes – Mrs Eagle's eyes
Sharpened beak, taloned claws
Strutting down the corridors
Eyes, eyes – Mrs Eagle's eyes

Hypnotizing, mesmerizing, traumatizing
Most surprising
Magnifying, terrifying, spying, prying, mystifying
Scary eyes, starey eyes, ever-watchful wary eyes

Eyes, eyes . . .

X-ray eyes, death-ray eyes
Scanning-every-which-way eyes
Beady eyes, speedy eyes, greedy, needy, seedy eyes
Laser eyes, razor eyes, amazing-in-their-gazing eyes.

Eyes, eyes . . .

Nothing you can hide from – Mrs Eagle's eyes
When they are open wide – Mrs Eagle's eyes
Watching like a hawk – Mrs Eagle's eyes
Nobody dare talk – Mrs Eagle's eyes
Everything she sees – Mrs Eagle's eyes
Three sixty degrees – Mrs Eagle's eyes

Eyes, eyes . . .

MR SHADOW'S SHOES

Mr Shadow's shoes
Soft-soled shoes

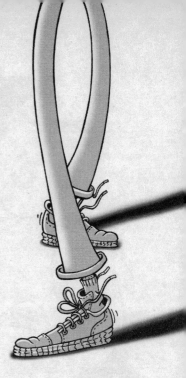

Shush shush – left and right
Shush shush – out of sight

Mr Shadow's always there
No one knows exactly where
Soft-soled shoes
Silent on the stairs

Shush shush – left and right
Shush shush – out of sight

He's sneaking and he's creeping
He's spying and he's peeping
Soft-soled shoes
Are what he keeps his feet in

Shush shush – left and right
Shush shush – out of sight

Like a whisper near the door
Ghostly in the corridor
Soft-soled shoes
Slide across the floor

Shush shush – left and right
Shush shush – out of sight

Mr Shadow's shoes
Soft-soled shoes
Soft-soled silent shoes
Soft-soled slippy shoes
Soft-soled slidy shoes
Mr Shadow's soft-soled slippy
      slidy silent shoes.

Shush shush – left and right
Shush shush – out of sight

Ssh – ssh – ssh – ssh – ssh – ssh

HUNGRY TEACHERS

Eating sweets in class you should not do
And you know the teachers do it too
The sweets they took weren't wasted
Your sweets they took and tasted
And now the teacher's tongues are all bright blue

FALSE FLOWER POWER

Our short-sighted teacher Mrs Bowes
Thought my plastic flower was a rose
She bent down to sniff and smell
You should have seen her leap and yell
When the water squirted up her nose

WRIGGLEBUM JOHN

Wrigglebum John, Wrigglebum John
He's got a chair that he can't sit on

Fidget left, fidget right
Fidget through the day and the night

Wrigglebum John, Wrigglebum John
He's got a chair that he can't sit on

Every day, hour and minute
He's got a chair but he can't stay in it

On the table watch him crawl
Climbing up and down the wall
Swinging from the lights and curtain
Of one thing you can be certain
Jumping, running, skipping, hopping
You have not a chance of stopping

Wrigglebum John, Wrigglebum John
He's got a chair that he can't sit on

Now he's here, now he's gone
Where does he get his energy from?

Wrigglebum, Wrigglebum, Wrigglebum John
Wrigglebum, Wrigglebum, Wrigglebum . . . JOHN!

BILLY DOESN'T LIKE SCHOOL REALLY

Billy doesn't like school really
It's not because he can't do the work
But because some of the other kids
Don't seem to like him that much

They call him names
And make up jokes about his mum

Everyone laughs . . . except Billy
Everyone laughs . . . except Billy

They all think it's okay
Because it's only a laugh and a joke
And they don't really mean it anyway
But Billy doesn't know that

And because of that
Billy doesn't like school really

ALL I WANT IS A FRIEND

All I want is a friend the little girl said
A friend to sit with me in class
A friend to have dinner with
A friend to talk about last night's telly with

All I want is a friend she said
As she sat down next to someone who didn't really
    like her

MISS SMITH'S MYTHICAL BAG

The curse of every class she'll see
No one knows its history
Its origin's a mystery
. . . Miss Smith's Mythical Bag

Beyond our understanding
You dare not put your hand in
The bag that keeps expanding
. . . Miss Smith's Mythical Bag

Broken chalk, a thousand pens
Red ink that's congealed
Forgotten fungus-covered bread
Mouldy orange peel
Lost car keys and headache pills
A Roman spear and shield
Football cards and marbles
The goalposts from the field

Where she goes it follows
All rippling lumps and hollows
The strangest things it swallows
. . . Miss Smith's Mythical Bag

With a menacing unzipped grin it's
From the Outer Limits
There are black holes deep within it
. . . Miss Smith's Mythical Bag

Crinkled tissues, Blu-tack balls, disfigured paper clips
Sweets all covered up with fluff, dried-up fibre-tips
Lumps of powdered milk and coffee
Last year's fish and chips
From the Triangle in Bermuda –
Several missing ships

Sometimes you hear it groan
Beyond the twilight zone
Make sure you're not alone
. . . Miss Smith's Mythical Bag

Shape-shifting, changing sizes
The bag she never tidies
It metamorphosizes
. . . Miss Smith's Mythical Bag

More mysterious than Loch Ness
It's from the Fifth Dimension
Stranger than an alien race
Beyond our comprehension
Brooding with a strange intent
That no one wants to mention
You'd better pay attention or you'll be in detention

With Miss Smith's mythical, metaphysical
Astronomical, gastronomical, anatomical
Clinical, cynical bag!

THE WHOOPEE CUSHION WAITING ON THE TEACHER'S CHAIR

All the class is silent
Our eyes are fixed on where
The whoopee cushion's waiting on our teacher's chair

First she paces to the right, then paces to the left
Carries on the lesson while perching on her desk
Nobody is moving, everybody stares
At the whoopee cushion waiting on our teacher's chair

We're praying for that moment
When she will sit down
Thinking of the giggling
When we hear that funny sound
SQUEAK! BLART! HONK!
FLURP! PARP! BLURRR!
The whoopee cushion's waiting on our teacher's chair

What's that noise – bouncing down the corridor
Mr Springer's coming – bouncing on the floor
We'd better all watch out, we'd better all beware
The whoopee cushion's waiting on our teacher's chair

He's going to sit down on it!
Oh no – disaster!
We're going to get in trouble now
With our big headmaster
It sounds like twenty tubas
Or a trumpet fanfare
You should have seen him jump
Ten feet in the air!
A red-faced ranting raver
He began to swear
Sounds that shook the ground
Vibrating everywhere
Sounds that bounced around
From behind his derrière
When the cushion was deflating
On the teacher's chair

Everyone is frightened now
We're bound to get detention
But what happens next
Is beyond our comprehension
Mr Springer turns to Miss and with an icy glare
He blames her for the whoopee cushion
On the teacher's chair

Twice the embarrassment, twice the fun
Got two teachers for the price of one!
So much pleasure for us all to share . . .
Thanks to the whoopee cushion
On the teacher's chair

DO AS YOU ARE TOLD! (TEACHERS)

LOTS OF CARROT CAKES

Apples, oranges and pears
Bananas, grapes everywhere
Lots of fruit and veg to share
Healthy in the classroom
The pupils have a healthy way
Five fresh portions every day
No matter what the teachers say
It's different in the staffroom

CAKES, CAKES, CAKES
LOTS OF CARROT CAKES

There's fruit there too it must be told
It's in the corner, five weeks old
Congealing in a bowl of mould
Not like in the classroom
Lots of biscuits in a box
Lots of cakes and lots of chocs
Always keeping up the stocks
Of sugar for the staffroom

CAKES, CAKES, CAKES . . .

Tins and tins and tins of sweets
Chocolate bars and cream–cake treats
Heroes, Roses, Quality Street
When staff are on their breaks
Flapjacks, fancies, jam and scones
Doughnuts piled up by the tons
Go on they say *I'll just have one*
Then dive into the cakes

CAKES, CAKES, CAKES . . .

They chomp and chew, dribble and slurp
Spilling cream on children's work
Lick their fingers, then they burp
The staffroom is a riot
Every week come what may
Always a member of staff's birthday
And even then the teachers say
I shouldn't – I'm on a diet
Go on then – I'll try it
Better keep it quiet
At Fat Club I'll just deny it!

CAKES, CAKES, CAKES . . .

They tut and lick their lips and say
I can't – I've had my points today
It's a green day anyway
Then change their minds – just like that
It sounds healthy so they take
A massive wodge of carrot cake
As carrots do not put on weight
It's cakes that make you fat!

CAKES, CAKES, CAKES . . .

EPITAPH FOR THE LAST MARTIAN

Crash-landing caused extinction
For the last of the Martian species
Here and here . . . and here and here
He rests in pieces.

WHY IS A BOTTOM CALLED A BOTTOM?

If the bottom of my body
Is that bit that's on the ground
Why is my bottom called my bottom
When it's only halfway down?

YOO-HOO, SWEETHEART!
GIVE YOUR NAN A KISS!

YOO-HOO, SWEETHEART!
GIVE YOUR NAN A KISS!

Nan has come to stay a while
When she tries to kiss me I'll
Grit my teeth and try to smile
There's no chance of that!
There is just one thing I dread
Lipstick smudges on my head
I'd rather just shake hands instead . . .
There's no chance of that – it's . . .

YOO-HOO, SWEETHEART!
GIVE YOUR NAN A KISS!

Then she starts to twist and tweak
Squeeze the skin upon my cheek
Does she give me chance to speak?
There's no chance of that!
She won't leave me on my own
Telling me how much I've grown
Will I get some time alone?
There's no chance of that – it's . . .

YOO-HOO, SWEETHEART!
GIVE YOUR NAN A KISS!

It's not right and it's not fair
You'd better watch out, you'd better beware
Will she shave her moustache hair?
There's no chance of that!
She's all hairs and no grace
When she stoops to kiss my face
Will her false teeth stay in place?
There's no chance of that – it's . . .

YOO-HOO, SWEETHEART!
GIVE YOUR
NAN A KISS!

THE JUMPER GRANNY KNITTED

The wool is rough and itchy
One sleeve is longer than the other
Teddies on the back
She thinks I am my little brother
It's shapeless and untrendy
Embarrassing, ill-fitted
I'm not going out like that . . .
In the jumper Granny knitted

Thomas the Tank Engine on the front
Seventeen shades of green
She thinks that I'm still seven
When really I'm thirteen
Every Christmas, every birthday
She really is committed
I'm not going out like that . . .
In the jumper Granny knitted

Don't worry you'll grow into it
It's the size of a family tent
And I was so much looking forward
To the present that she sent
Pretend that it's just perfect
And smile while teeth are gritted
I'm not going out like that . . .
In the jumper Granny knitted

No way seen in public
For fear of ridicule
Too much humiliation
And never near my school
But whenever Granny comes to call
However wits are pitted
I'm not going out like that . . .
In the jumper Granny knitted

I'm not going out like that
In the jumper Granny knitted
I'd rather go in hiding
But that is not permitted
You always have to wear it once
Or you may as well admit it . . .
That you hate and cannot stand
It makes you want to vomit and
You'd rather have one second-hand
Than . . . the jumper Granny knitted
I'm not going out like that
In the jumper Granny knitted!

STEPMOTHER

Life with her is a fairy tale
She's not like any other
Totally ace and magically cool
My wicked stepmother

STRANGE RHYMING FACTS ABOUT SOME OF MY FRIENDS

My friend Jim is skinny and thin
My friend Dave is starting to shave
My friend Don has no trousers on
My friend Neville – cheeky devil!

My friend Stan is my biggest fan
My friend Michael rides his unicycle
My friend Stu spends hours in the loo
My friend Billy wears pants that are frilly!

My friend Mark – he glows in the dark
My friend Brian can burp like a lion
Perhaps you have rhymes about some of your friends
Write them all down so this poem ends!

WISH LIST FOR THE BULLY IN YOUR LIFE

I wish you nasty illnesses
Like mumps and chickenpox
I wish you nice surprises
Like scorpions hiding in your socks

I hope that you get locked inside
The snake cage at the zoo
I hope your dog has diarrhoea
In your favourite shoe

I'd like to think of you dressed in
A tutu pink and bright
While playing for the rugby team
With fairy wings so white

May all your teeth fall out at once
May head lice love your hair
May wasps infest your underpants
Sting everything in there

May your nose be always running
May you suffer from BO
May flies and skunks surround you
Wherever you may go

I wish you crusty pimples
And bad breath every day
I wish – I wish – I wish – I wish
I wish you'd go away!

THE AMAZING CAPTAIN CONCORDE

5 4 3 2 1 . . . BLAST OFF!

Is it a bird? Is it a plane?
Look at the size of the nose on his face!
Is it a bird? Is it a plane?
Captain Concorde is his name!
Captain Concorde NEEOWN!
What a big nose NEEOWN!

He's a man with a mission
Radar vision
A nose that's supersonic
Faster than the speed of sound
His Y-fronts are bionic

Is it a bird? Is it a plane?
Look at the size of the nose on his face!
Is it a bird? Is it a plane?
Captain Concorde is his name!
Captain Concorde NEEOWN!
What a big nose NEEOWN!

Anytime anyplace anywhere
But never ever Mondays
Cos that's the day the Captain's mum
Washes his red undies
Anytime anyplace anywhere
His power is fantastic
Everything's under control
With super-strength elastic!
Anytime anywhere anyplace
But the bathrooms is a no no
Cos the toilet seat his teeth! OW!
And then it's time to go so . . .

Is it a bird? Is it a plane?
Look at the size of the nose on his face!
Is it a bird? Is it a plane?
Captain Concorde is his name!
Captain Concorde NEEOWN!
What a big nose NEEOWN!

The Amazing Captain Concorde . . . he's a superman
The Amazing Captain Concorde . . . super underpants

Who's the man with the supersonic nose?
    Captain Concorde!
Who's the man with the terrible taste in clothes?
    Captain Concorde!
Who's the man who always helps his mum?
    Captain Concorde!
Who's the man you'd like to become?
    Captain Concorde!

Is it a bird? Is it a plane?
Look at the size of the nose on his face!
Is it a bird? Is it a plane?
Captain Concorde is his name!
Captain Concorde NEEOWN!
What a big nose NEEOWN!

THE TWELVE LEFTOVERS OF CHRISTMAS

On the twelfth day of Christmas
I found upon the floor . . .

12 sprouts a-hiding
11 toys a-broken
10 cardboard boxes
9 lights not working
8 dented baubles
7 mince pies moulding
6 tins of biscuits
5 – PAIRS – OF – SOCKS!
4 cards unposted
3 selection boxes
2 sacks of paper
And a turkey we couldn't quite eat

THE POPPY RED –
LEST EVER WE FORGET

Bravery we cannot comprehend
Passing time does not the sorrow mend
Battles that we do not understand
We pray there's no return to no-man's-land
The heroes that we never met
The poppy red – lest ever we forget

Those memories forever will remain
We pray will not tread that path again
Too many lost and gone so we may live
Remembrance – all that we can give
We never can repay their debt
The poppy red – lest ever we forget

In Flanders Fields, the trenches and Dunkirk
When evil hums then good must do its work
Their sacrifice lives on eternally
Their inspiration and their dignity
Dulce et decorum est
The poppy red – lest ever we forget

A century on and still we shall recall
With heart and soul we now salute you all
And recognize those lives that went before
And pray that peace may conquer any war
So let us join as one and pay respect
The poppy red – lest ever we forget

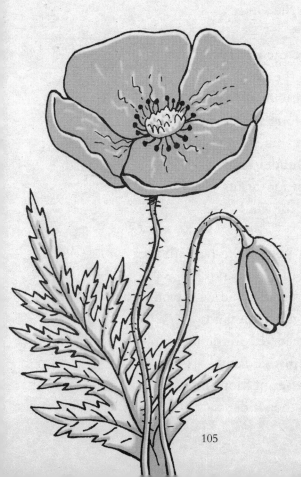

FOOTPRINTS IN THE SAND

Footprints, footprints
Footprints in the sand
You and me, Lord, on the beach
Walking hand in hand
Side by side you walk with me
Through this barren land
Footprints, footprints
Footprints in the sand

I look and see the footprints
Footprints in the sand
Two souls entwined together
God's walk along with man
Then I glance and see a sight
I don't quite understand
Just one set of footprints
Footprints in the sand

You said that you would be with me
I followed your command
But you left me all alone with pain
That I could not withstand
The time I needed you the most
My Lord, I must demand
Why just one set of footprints
Footprints in the sand?

The Lord looked down and smiled
With gentle reprimand
My son, this explanation
Everything is planned
I never left your side at all
And when you could not stand
That was when I carried you
Those footprints in the sand

Footprints, footprints
Footprints in the sand
You and me, Lord, on the beach
Walking hand in hand
Often you would carry me
Through this barren land
Footprints, footprints
Footprints in the sand

THESE ARE THE HANDS

These are the hands that wave
These are the hands that clap
These are the hands that pray
These are the hands that tap

These are the hands that grip
These are the hands that write
These are the hands that paint
These are the hands that fight

These are the hands that hug
These are the hands that squeeze
These are the hands that point
These are the hands that tease

These are the hands that take
These are the hands that poke
These are the hands that give
These are the hands that stroke

These are the hands that hold
These are the hands that love
These are the hands of mine
That fit me like a glove

WHAT IS A MERMAID MADE OF?

Glittering shells, rainbow scales
The shimmer and glimmer of angelfish tails
The glow of a jellyfish, grace of a whale

The wishes of fishes, a breath of sea breeze
Seven blue shades from seven blue seas
A mermaid is made from a mixture of these

MISTER RANDALL'S SANDALS

Mister Randall's sandals
They're ancient and they're old
Battered, torn and tattered
And always open-toed
Weathered leather from whenever
They just look a shambles
Don't look now, don't look down
At Mister Randall's sandals

Mister Randall's sandals
Loved by CSI
You can tell just where he's been
And what he's done and why
Evidence for all to see
All mystery untangles
There's history, geology
In Mister Randall's sandals

Mister Randall's sandals
There's glue and drawing pins
Chewing gum and squished and squashed up
Blu-tack moulded in
Buckles jingle-jangle
As the ancient thread untangles
Coffee stains and lunch remains
On Mister Randall's sandals

Mister Randall's sandals
Lumpy, chunky toes
The toenails that he never cuts
And the mould and where it grows
Toadstools lurk in the dirt and the murk
And the mushrooms grow at angles
Blink your eyes as the gases rise
From Mister Randall's sandals

Mister Randall's sandals
Observe the yellow skin
But where do the sandals end
And where do his feet begin?
The skin and leather – joined together
Like waxy melted candles
The leather's dried – the skin has died
On Mister Randall's sandals

Mister Randall's sandals
His hairy hobbit feet
The gases that they're giving off
Like rancid cheesy meat
Fungus fumes foul every room
As the stink takes hold and strangles
Hold your nose when you're near the toes
Of Mister Randall's sandals

WHEN THE WASP FLEW UP MY BROTHER'S SHORTS

A family fun-filled holiday
Seaside football – match of the day
On the beach the score nine–nine
When the match went into injury time
We soon forgot our day for sports
When the wasp flew up my brother's shorts!

We misread that situation
Thought it was his celebration
Scoring a goal – dancing about
The yell, the scream, the twist and shout
We're all smiles as he cavorts
When the wasp flew up my brother's shorts

The moves he made we'll never forget
The bottom wiggle, the pirouette
The somersaults and acrobatics
A million amateur dramatics
Out of control and out of sorts
When the wasp flew up my brother's shorts

When the wasp flew up my brother's shorts
His eyes bulge wide and his face distorts
Worried where that wasp is caught
Scared of the sting, his body contorts
But the wasp was the one that was most distraught

Up one leg then down the other
Relief for the wasp, relief for my brother
Took them both a while to recover
Panic attacks and flashback thoughts . . .
When the wasp flew up my brother's shorts

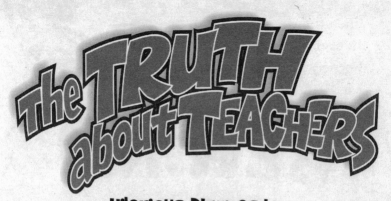

The TRUTH about TEACHERS

Hilarious Rhymes by
Paul Cookson, David Harmer
Brian Moses and Roger Stevens

Can you bear to know the whole truth about
teachers? They all have middle names, you
know, and hobbies, pets and favourite bands.
They enjoy themselves at the weekend. They
have fun inside the staffroom. All in all, there's
a lot more going on with your mild-mannered
maths teacher than you might imagine . . .

IT'S BEHIND YOU!

MONSTER POEMS BY PAUL COOKSON AND DAVID HARMER

is a fantastic collection of very funny
monster poems from two bestselling poets.

Find out what to do if there's a monster under your bed,
a zombie in the garden or a cyclops at your school.
Beware the mighty Sockodile and the Death Kiss
Suction Grandma Leeches, and if you see a
Mutant Vampire Teacher . . .
run for your life . . .

ILLUSTRATED BY CARL FLINT